# 42
# Mandala Patterns
## COLORING BOOK

**Wolfgang Hund**

Hunter House PUBLISHERS
Alameda, CA

D1737380

## Ordering

Trade bookstores in the U.S. and Canada please contact:

> Publishers Group West
> 1700 Fourth Street, Berkeley CA 94710
> Phone: (800) 788-3123   Fax: (510) 528-3444

Hunter House books are available at bulk discounts for textbook course adoptions; to qualifying community, health care, and government organizations; and for special promotions and fund-raising. For details please contact:

> Special Sales Department
> Hunter House Inc., PO Box 2914, Alameda CA 94501-0914
> Phone: (510) 865-5282   Fax: (510) 865-4295
> E-mail: ordering@hunterhouse.com

Individuals can order our books from most bookstores, by calling toll-free (800) 266-5592, or from our website at www.hunterhouse.com

## Project Credits

Illustrations: Wolfgang Hund

Translator: André Kuehnemund

Acquisitions Editor: Jeanne Brondino

Editorial & Production Assistant: Emily Tryer

Publicity Manager: Sara Long

Customer Service Manager: Christina Sverdrup

Administrator: Theresa Nelson

Publisher: Kiran S. Rana

Cover Design & Book Production: Jil Weil

Copy Editors: Kiran Rana, Alexandra Mummery

Associate Editor: Alexandra Mummery

Acquisitions & Publicity Assistant: Lori Covington

Sales & Marketing Assistant: Earlita K. Chenault

Order Fulfillment: Joel Irons

Computer Support: Peter Eichelberger

Printed and bound by Bang Printing, Brainerd, Minnesota

Manufactured in the United States of America

9  8  7  6  5  4  3          First Edition          06  07  08  09

# An Introductory Note...

## Mandalas in Class: A Teacher's Dream Come True?

### "Once upon a time..."

It is 8:30 on a Monday morning in an urban middle school. Children are chasing each other in the hallways and the auditorium, playing softball, solving conflicts by fighting, playing jump rope, or just standing around their lockers chatting. New busloads of students arrive, and the children fill up the locker aisles before moving on to their classrooms.

In classroom 2A the chalkboard reads, "Choose one of these mandalas and get started." The teacher has laid out copies of five different mandalas on a table. In the background one can hear relaxing music. The first few children look at the different mandalas on the table, choose one, and go to their desks. They pull out their colored markers and start coloring in their mandalas.

It is now 8:40. Nobody is running around in the classroom anymore. Outside, one can still hear the muffled noises of the other students. Occasionally, a student enters the room, greets the teacher, goes to his desk, drops his backpack, walks to the front, chooses a mandala, and starts coloring. The 8:45 classroom bell does not cause any interruption. The teacher reduces the volume on the CD player every 5 minutes, and by 8:55 the room is completely silent. Even conversations about the weekend have died down completely, without the teacher having had to remind the students to be quiet.

*Mandalas, like the ones in this coloring book, have been used for relaxation, meditation, and recreation for centuries by people in many different cultures. In the following text we have suggested how mandalas can be used in the classroom by teachers and educators, but mandalas are for everyone to use and enjoy. We hope you will feel free to try out our suggestions at home, at work, or wherever you choose, and modify them creatively to suit your needs.*

The first students are finished coloring by 9:05. They sit back and look at their work. The teacher interrupts the remaining students without rushing them and tells them that although there is no more time to work on the mandalas now, during the next break from work they will be able to continue coloring where they left off. Some students may choose to take their mandalas home and finish them there. Eventually, though, all of the students' mandalas will be combined into a single large mural and put on the classroom wall as a visual representation of the tranquil feelings mandalas inspire.

Does this really sound like a fairy tale in today's hectic world? Is this an impossibility because of the overstimulation the media offers our children every day and each weekend?

Actually, the situation I have tried to describe above is what I experienced one morning with a group of students who had only encountered mandalas once before!

Certainly, this was not a problem school in an economically challenged area of a big city. It wasn't a high school either. But I think this activity would have worked in that type of setting too. Perhaps things would not unfold in exactly the same way, but the results would probably be similar.

Anybody who has seen even once how a lively, noisy, sometimes chaotic classroom (no matter what the age group or type of school) quiets down within a few moments and transforms into a pleasant, focused, concentrated group, will certainly include this tool in his or her repertoire as a teacher.

Later that same day, I received a business call from a colleague at a high school. He was, as always, stressed out and in a hurry. Toward the end of our conversation, he asked the usual polite questions: "So, how are you doing? What are you doing right now?" I answered that I was sitting at my desk, coloring a mandala. "You're doing *what???*" After a few minutes of surprise and total disbelief (should a teacher be coloring pictures? Especially during work hours?), he became very interested. Just the idea that mandalas can serve as an effective way to relax after a busy morning piqued his interest. Especially since a teacher needs to maintain his or her ability to function "at an optimal level"!

## Mandalas...the Cool, New Thing?

Those who have been teachers for any length of time have probably experienced how quickly the excitement over an innovative new method of instruction subsides. The techniques that survive are always the well-established ones that have proven successful in most situations in daily school life—and that suit differing individual teaching styles.

Mandalas have been trendy in Europe for quite some time—celebrated in New Age circles as a method for finding oneself and recommended as a therapeutic defense against stress and psychosomatic problems. The many books and articles written about them have led to these circle-motifs often being equated with esotericism and New Age psychology.

However, the fact of the matter is that mandalas are much older and more cross-cultural than the New Age movement. The round, stained-glass windows in gothic cathedrals prove that the soothing, reflective, and peaceful effect of this kind of composition has long been recognized in the Western world. The circle is a basic form both in nature and in culture. It automatically draws attention to its center and has therefore served as a thought-collecting and reflective aid since prehistoric times. It is this quality that can be used in the classroom to help children find both peace and quiet.

## Teaching Peace and Quiet

Quiet is a basic requirement for all children, a fact that Maria Montessori and others have emphasized.

By quiet I do not mean an external, forced absence of sound brought about by strict discipline. This only results in tension, conflicts, and restlessness. Rather I mean an inner peace in which the children can retreat into themselves, collect their thoughts, concentrate, and reflect; an inner composure that can only flourish in the appropriate atmosphere. It is the teacher's task to both create and retain this atmosphere, and to achieve this the teacher must be prepared to try something new. Using these mandalas in the classroom can create this type of quiet space for children.

# Different Ways of Using Mandalas

There are three main ways to use mandalas:

- looking at them
- coloring them in
- creating your own

The first two options can be carried out easily with a minimum of teacher preparation. I believe there should be no set ways for or rules about using mandalas in class, so the following suggestions are intentionally brief.

## Looking at Mandalas

- Project a colored mandala (e.g., a gothic stained-glass window) using a slide projector or an overhead projector (a colored-in overhead transparency).
- Look at the mandala as a group, either in silence or with suitable, relatively quiet background music.
- After several minutes of reflection, talk about the mandala (though this is not necessary).

- After showing the children a colored overhead, project a blank copy of the mandala and ask the children to think of their own colors. After about 3 minutes, give them a copy of the mandala to color in.

## Coloring-in Mandalas

- It would go against the aim of the exercise for children to have to color in a mandala that they don't like. For this reason, there should always be a selection from which they can choose.
- Make sure that the situation is suitable (that there is enough time, sufficient lighting, a sign on the classroom door...).
- Photocopy the mandalas onto white, 8.5" x 11"-sized paper (or larger, if possible).
- Different ways of doing the coloring are possible, experiment with them:
  — coloring individually;
  — coloring in pairs (enlarge the mandala onto larger paper); the children can work at the same time or take turns;
  — coloring in a group (enlarge the mandala onto even larger paper); not more than four children per group.
- Give various time limits:
  — have children work on their mandalas until everyone is finished (provide extra tasks for those who finish first);
  — give the children a certain time limit (at least 20 minutes), and have them finish their mandalas during free time;
  — have the coloring time spread out over the week (for complicated mandalas), color in one section every day in free time, before the lesson begins, or between lessons.
- A box of mandalas placed in the free-play area can provide children with an interesting new opportunity. This idea can be used at home, too (often the enthusiasm is passed onto the parents, who in turn learn to relax together with their children—not the worst thing that a school can achieve!).
- For a parents' evening—consider trying mandalas as a change of pace!
- While coloring in
  — there is silence and no talking (not even in pair or group work) and/or
  — there is music playing quietly in the background (classical music, meditative music, etc.).

- Not every part of the mandala has to be colored in; some parts can be left white intentionally.
- Provide art supplies for the children to use for coloring in the mandalas—as many different colors as possible:
    — felt pens/markers (bright/fluorescent colors)
    — colored pencils
    — water colors and crayons (for bigger mandalas)
    — a mixture of the above
- Choose the colors consciously (contrasting colors, color families or palettes, warm and/or cold colors, by feel) or by chance (with closed eyes).
- Pass the mandala on to another child after a certain period of time; after a while, hand it back or pass it on to other children—this provides the children with experience in sharing and cooperation.
- Usually mandalas are colored from the inside out, but the children should feel free to do as they please. There is no "right" or "wrong" way to color in a mandala!
- When the children have finished, they can hang their mandalas on the board or around the room. This creates a fascinating combination of pictures. To wrap up the event, look at all of the pictures as a group (in silence or with background music) and finally discuss them ("I like this one because...").
- The finished mandalas make a colorful wall decoration that will invite the viewer to absorb, relax, and even talk about it.

## Creating Your Own Mandalas

This is often the hardest part, because some children find it especially hard to draw on a blank piece of paper. Particularly in classrooms that have fairly strict settings, students often fear that they might do something "wrong" if they give into their moods and give free reign to their imaginations. Sadly, this inhibition is something that our children actually learn, and this learning process frequently happens for the very first time when they are in school.

Just as the mandala patterns in this book aren't perfect (they were handmade, using rulers and other tools, etc.), we shouldn't expect children to be able to draw a perfect, beautiful mandala. A first step could be providing half of a mandala to a child or at least a circle with a center point.

Whether one wants to or should first draw the outlines with a pencil, whether one should use rulers, masks, etc., or simply start drawing freehand using color pencils should be totally up to each individual. At the same time, you (as a teacher) should be able to draw a mandala relatively easily, and thereby encourage the children.

Something you might want to do (not at the very beginning, but after having done this for a little while) is to design mandalas that have a theme. This can be done with a partner or in groups, using themes like:

- Christmas/Easter/Halloween/the seasons
- Mother's Day/vacations
- plants/nature/flowers/trees
- triangles/squares/circles/spirals
- ...

If someone gets "stuck" while designing a mandala, it is sometimes a good plan to simply put it aside for a while and try again later. Often, the flow of ideas will suddenly reappear if you take a break.

So, to end this Introduction: Try it for yourself!
You will see that school can be fun—for students and teachers!

Wolfgang Hund
Hersbruck, Germany

# The Mandalas

1
2
3
4
5
6

7
8
9
10
11
12

13
14
15
16
17
18

19
20
21
22
23
24

25
26
27
28
29
30

31
32
33
34
35
36

37
38
39
40
41
42

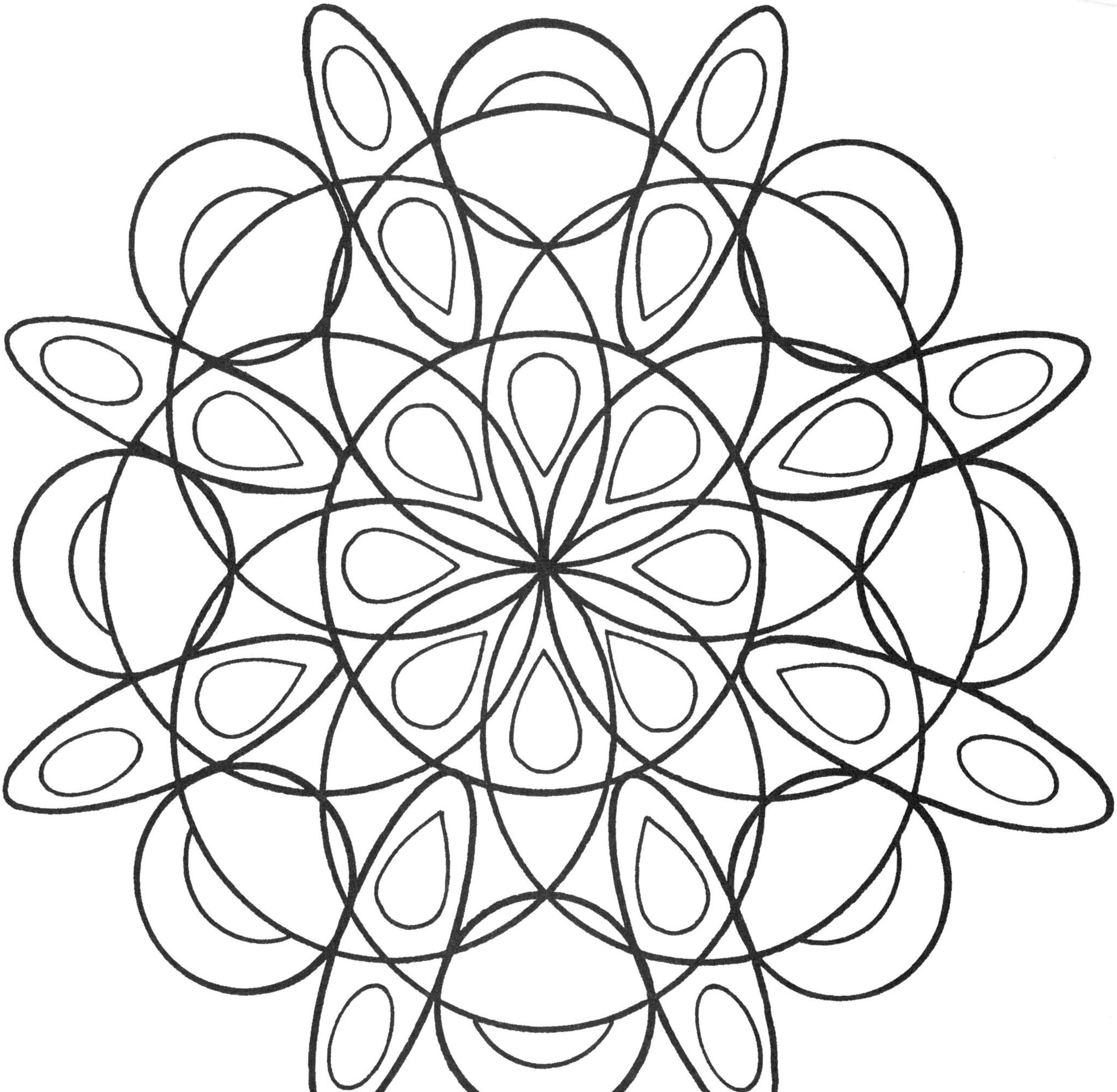

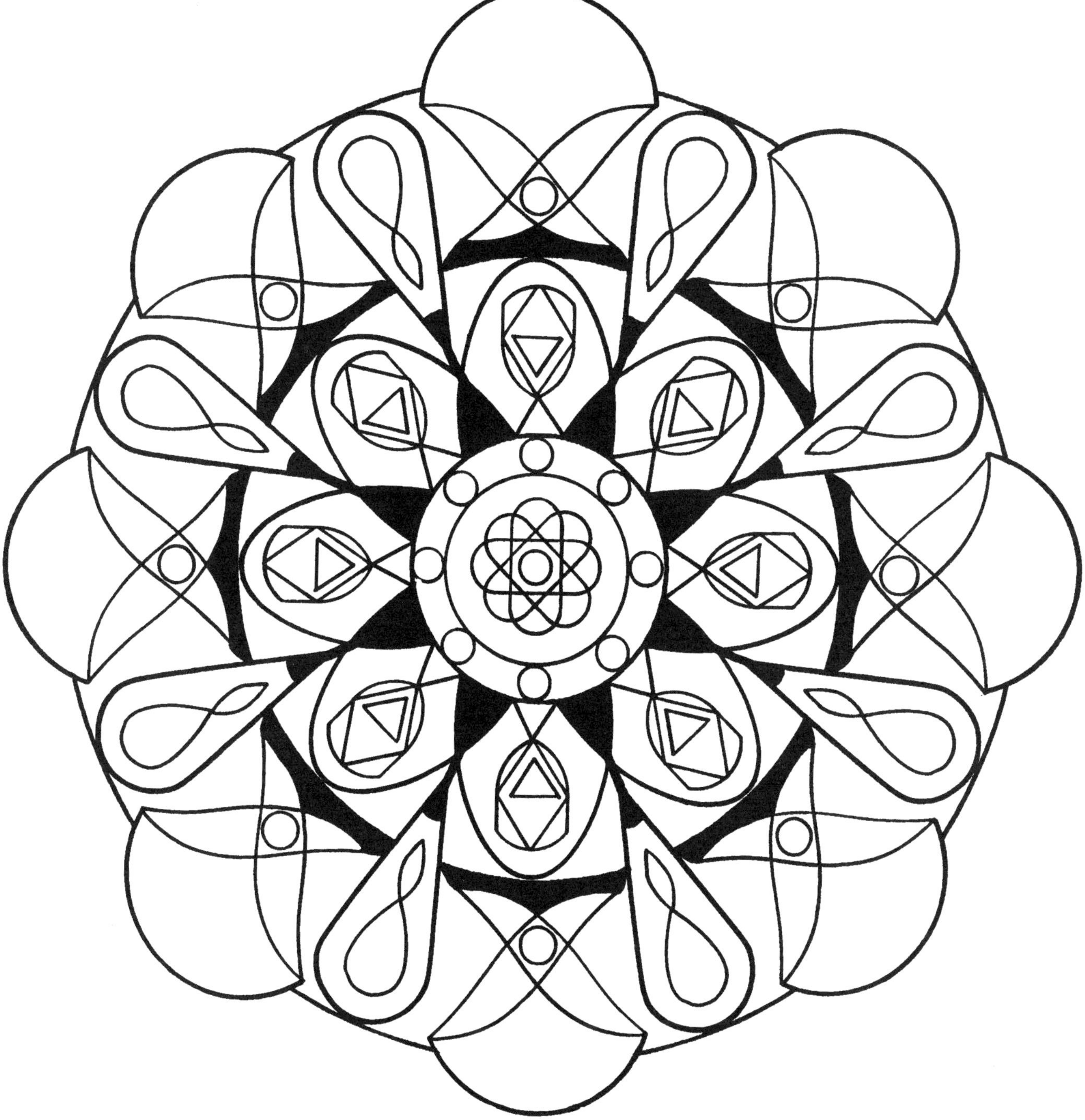

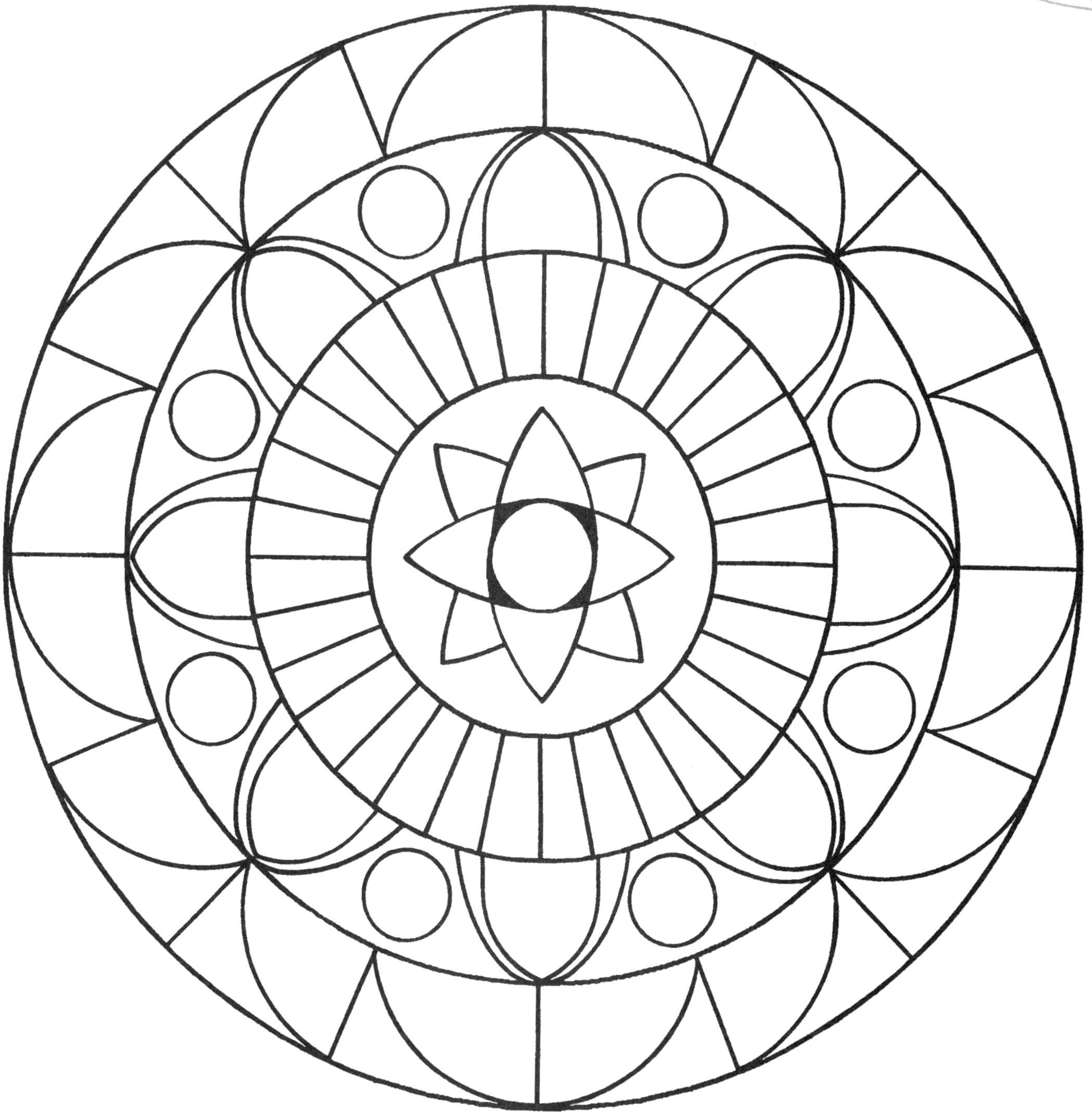

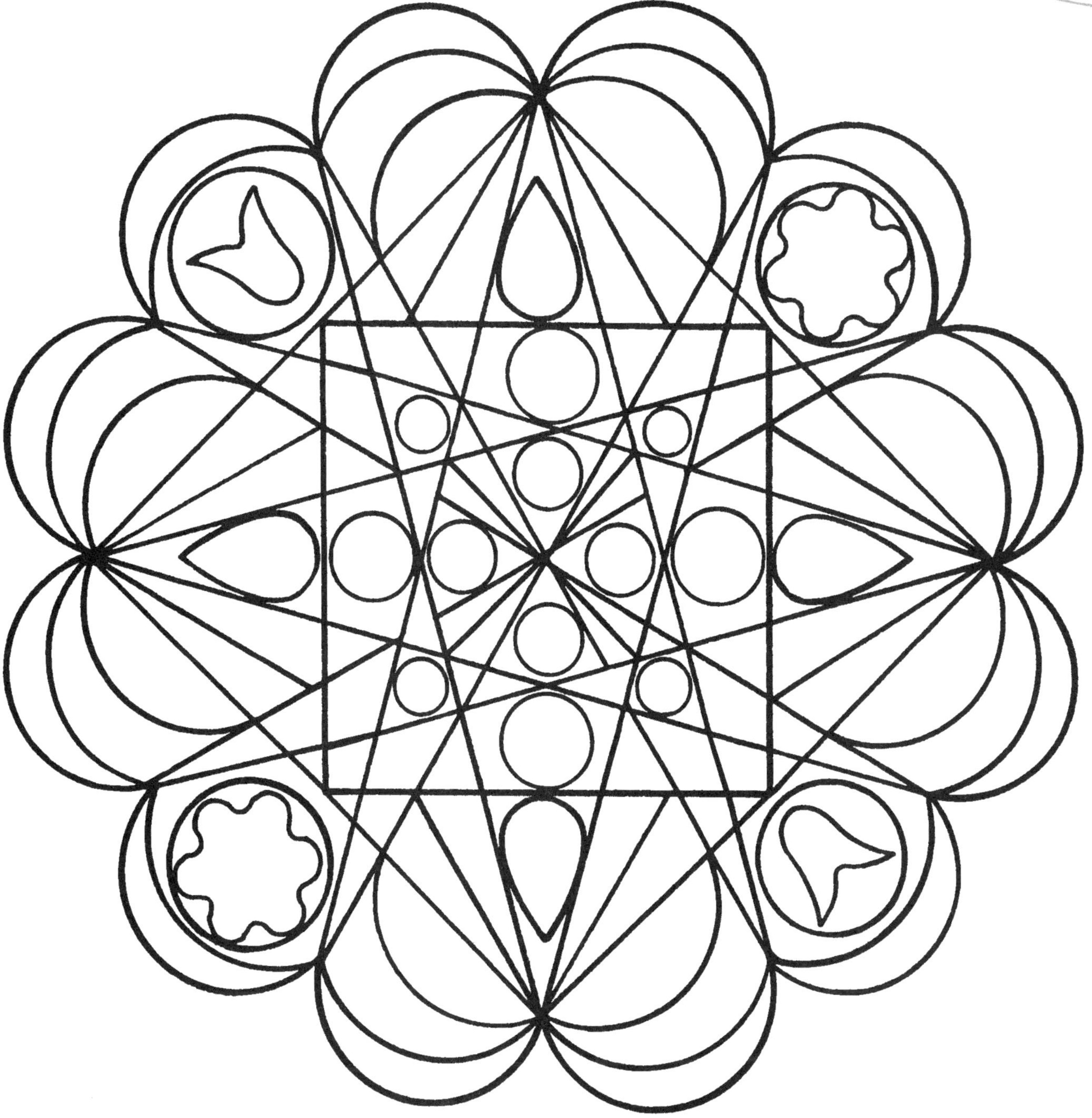

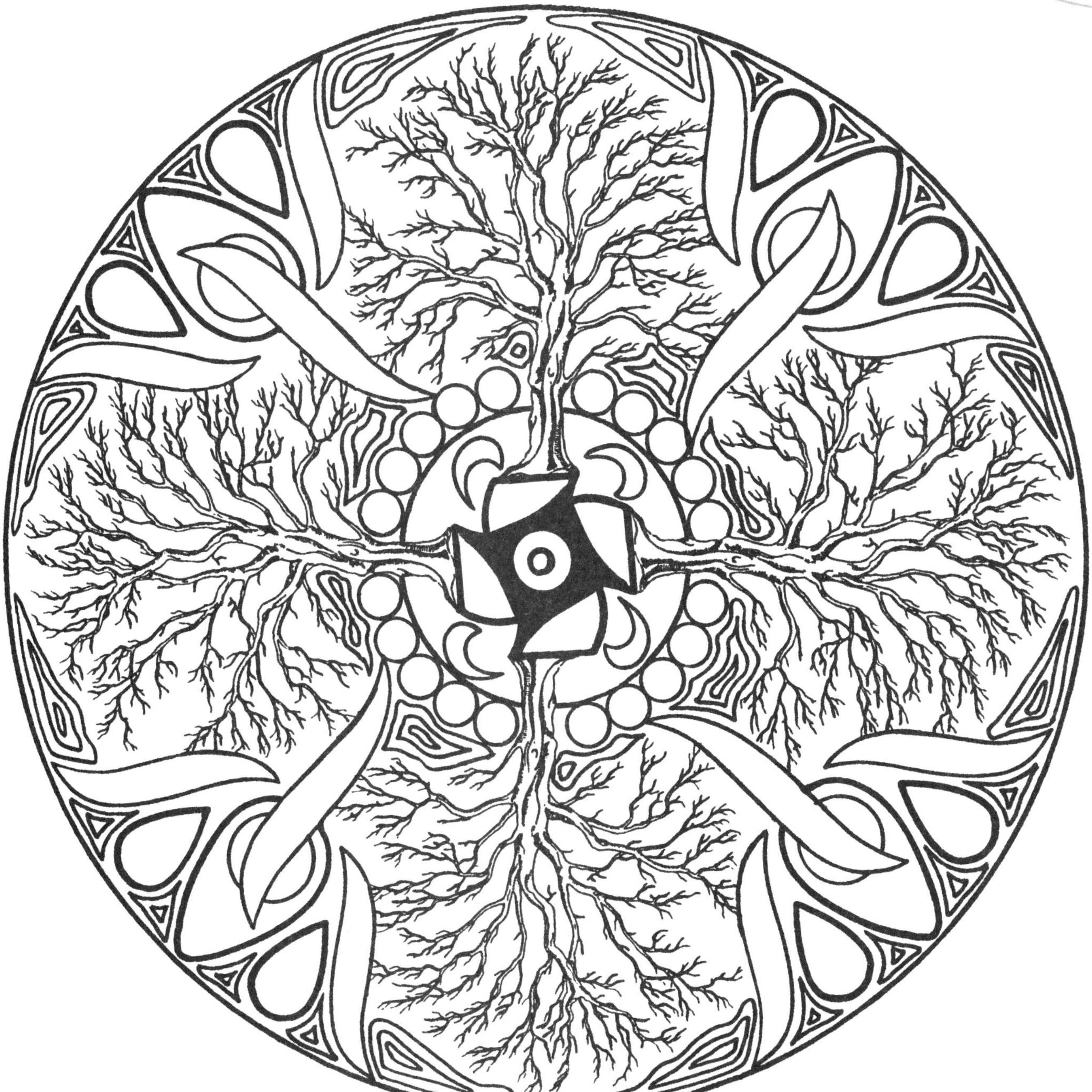

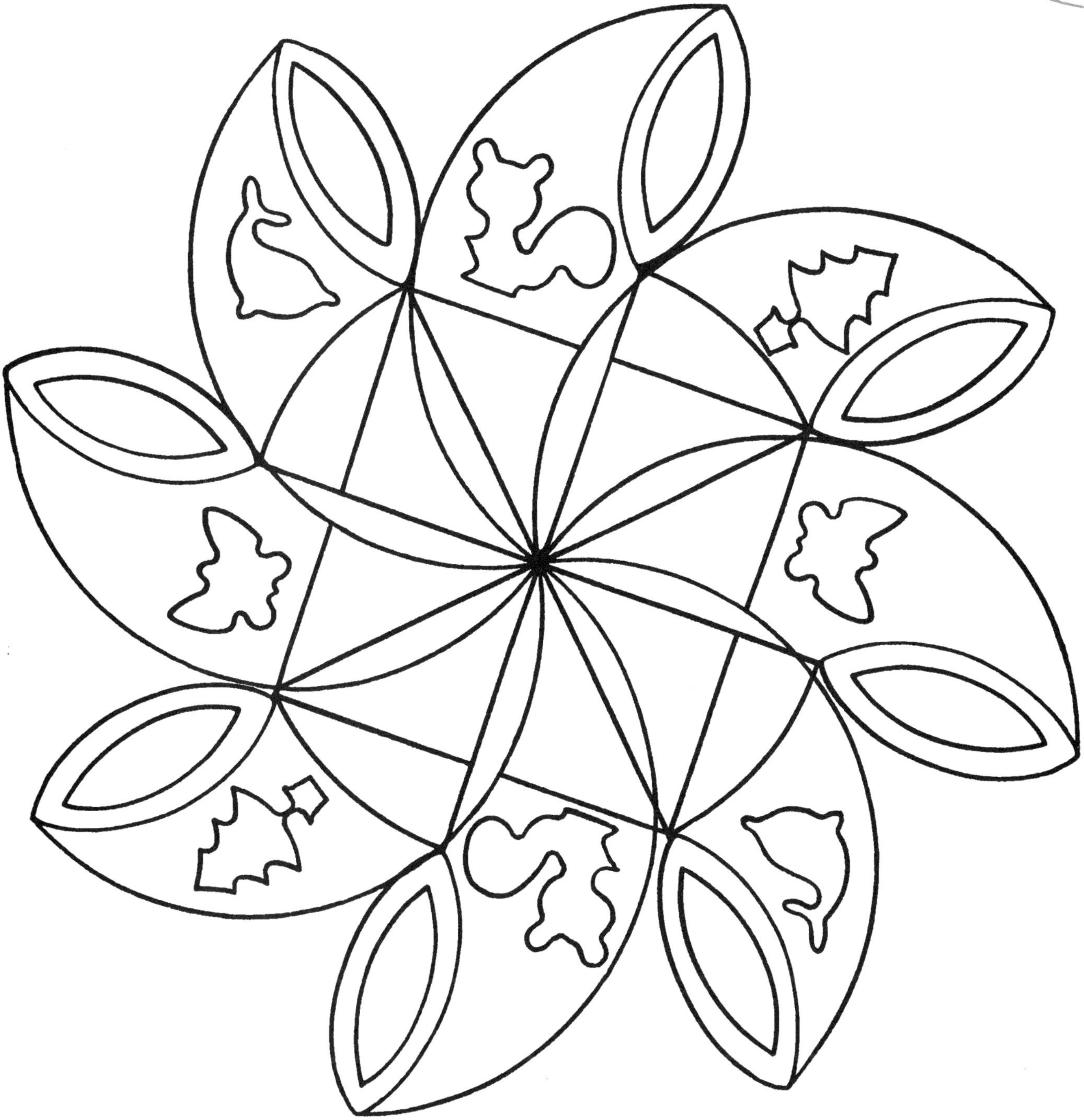

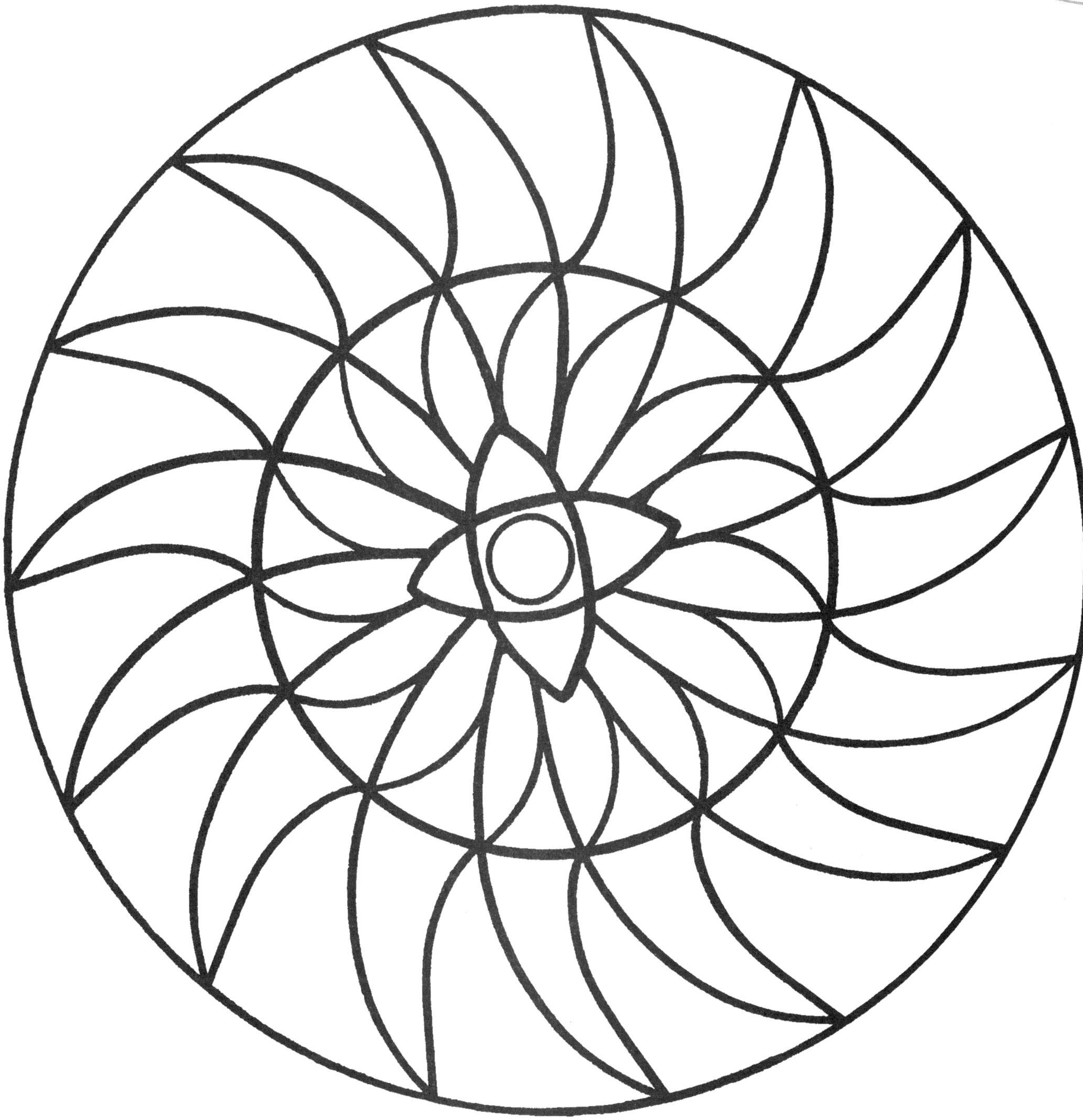

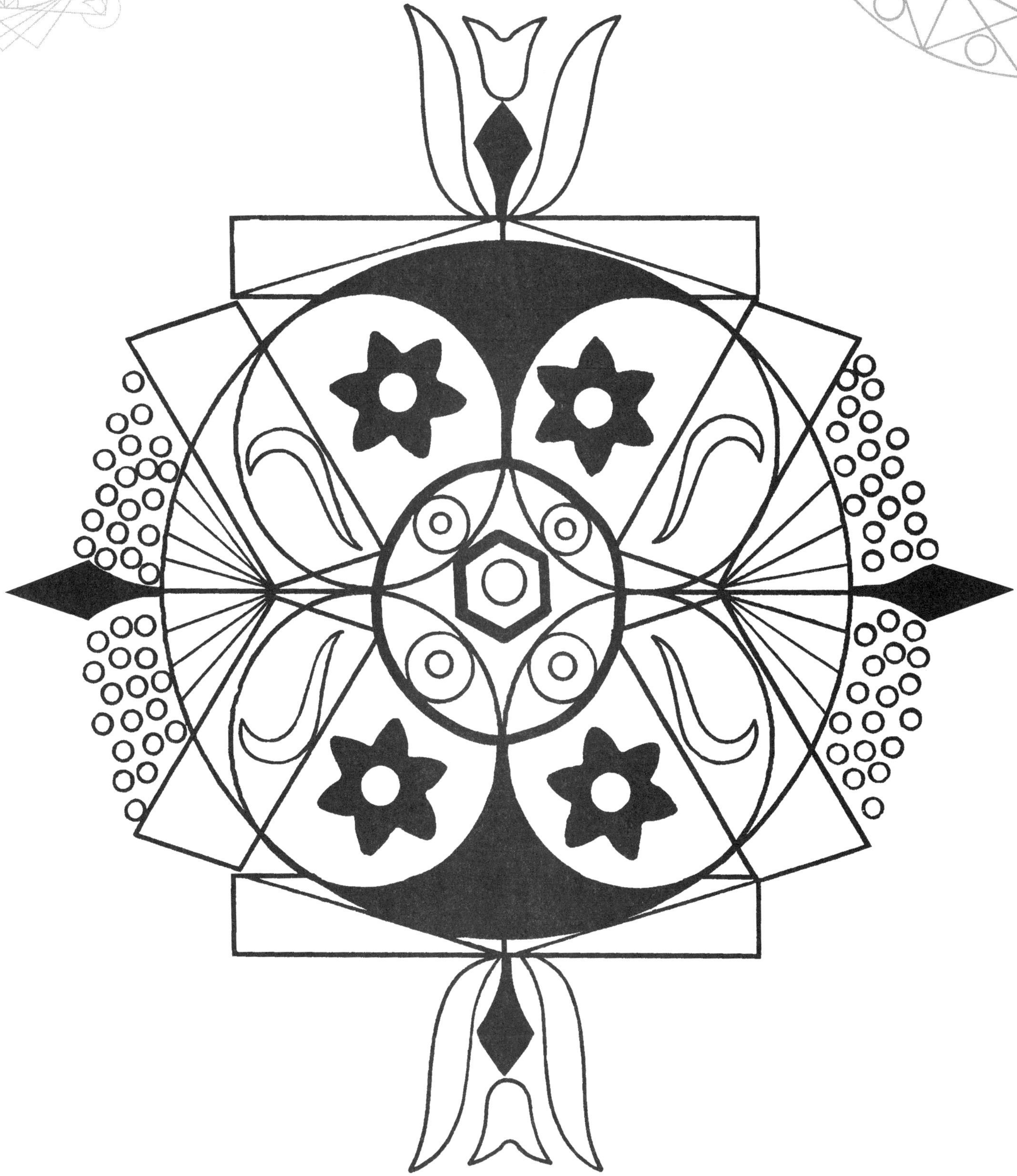

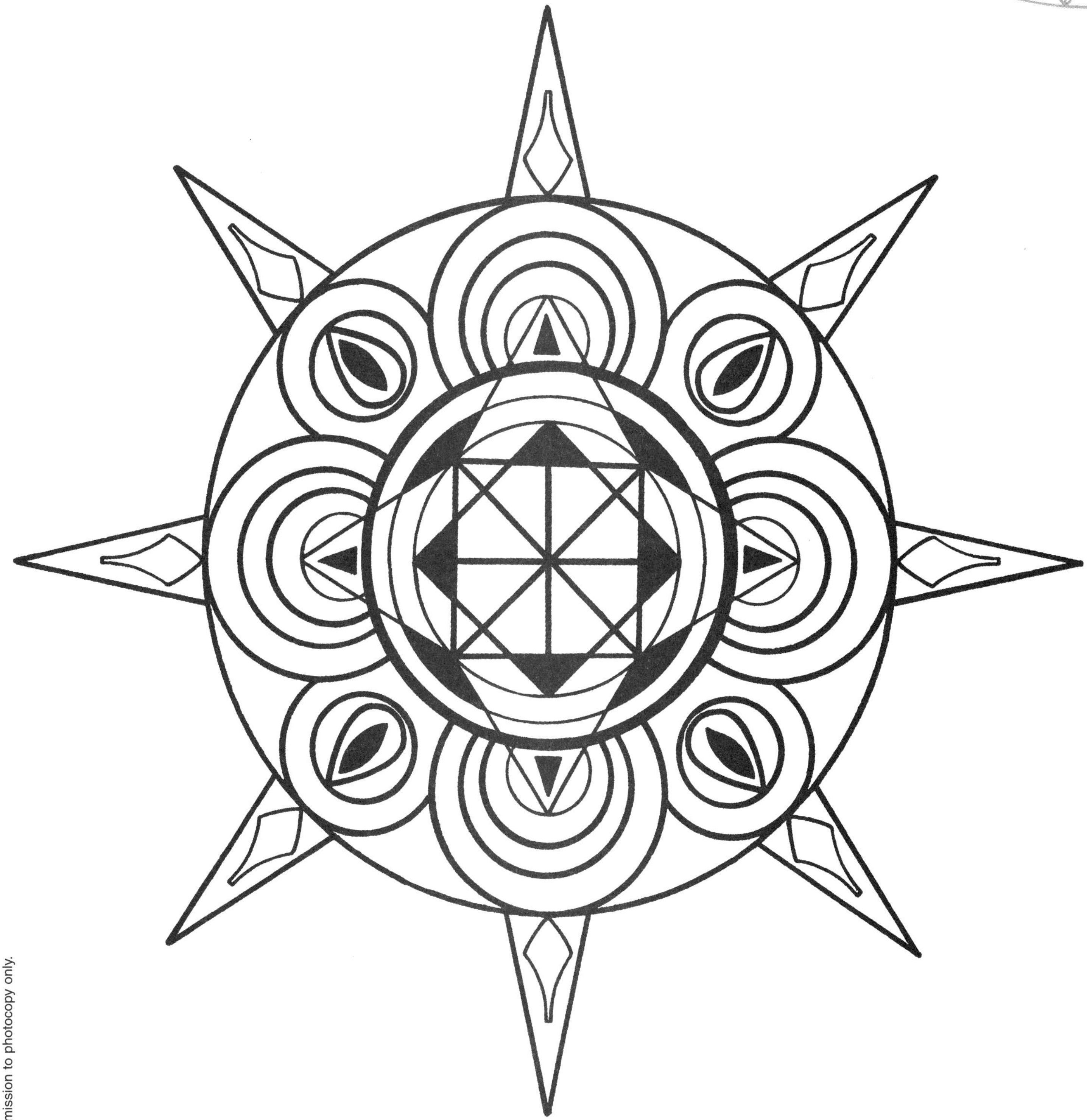

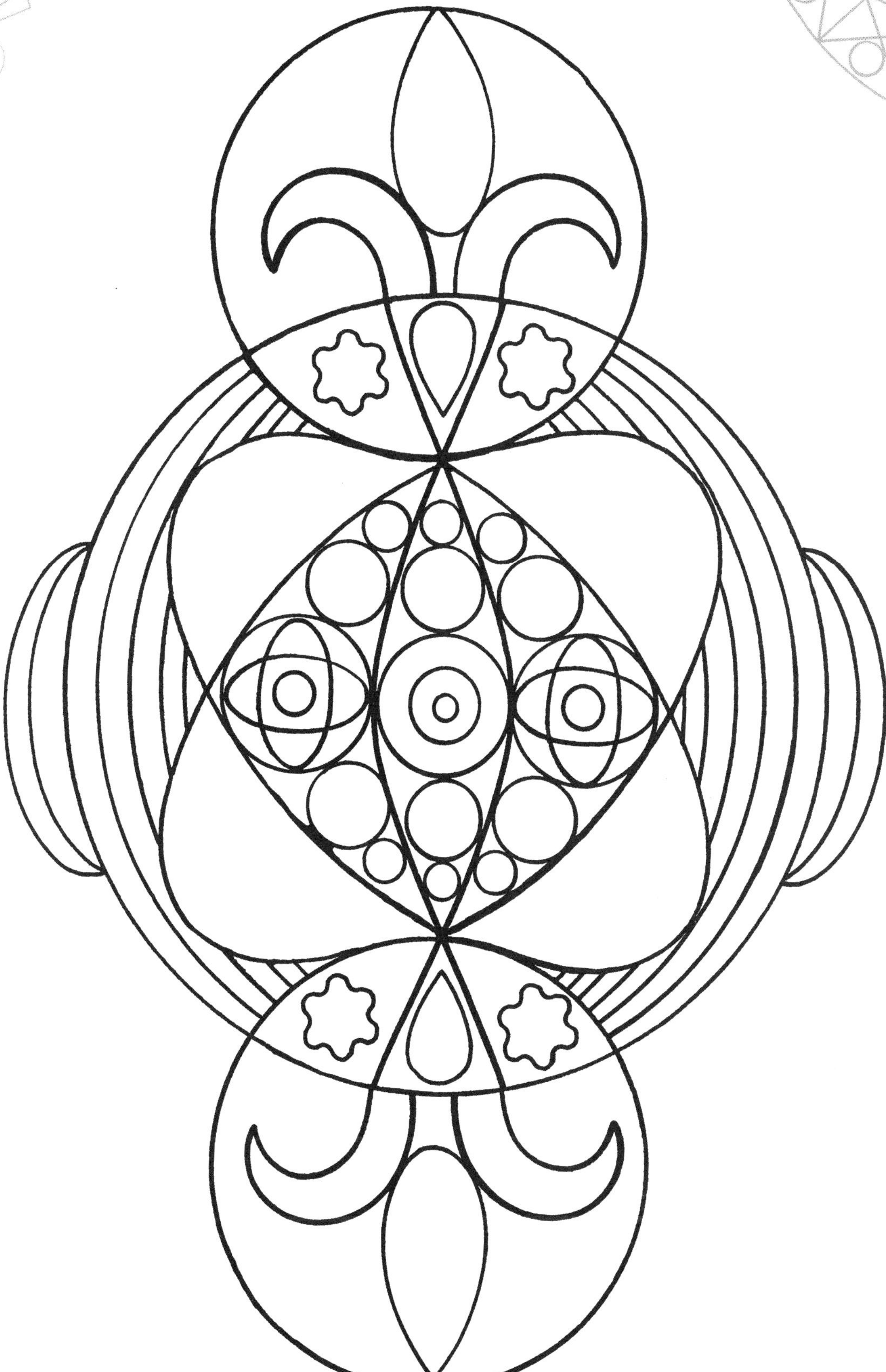

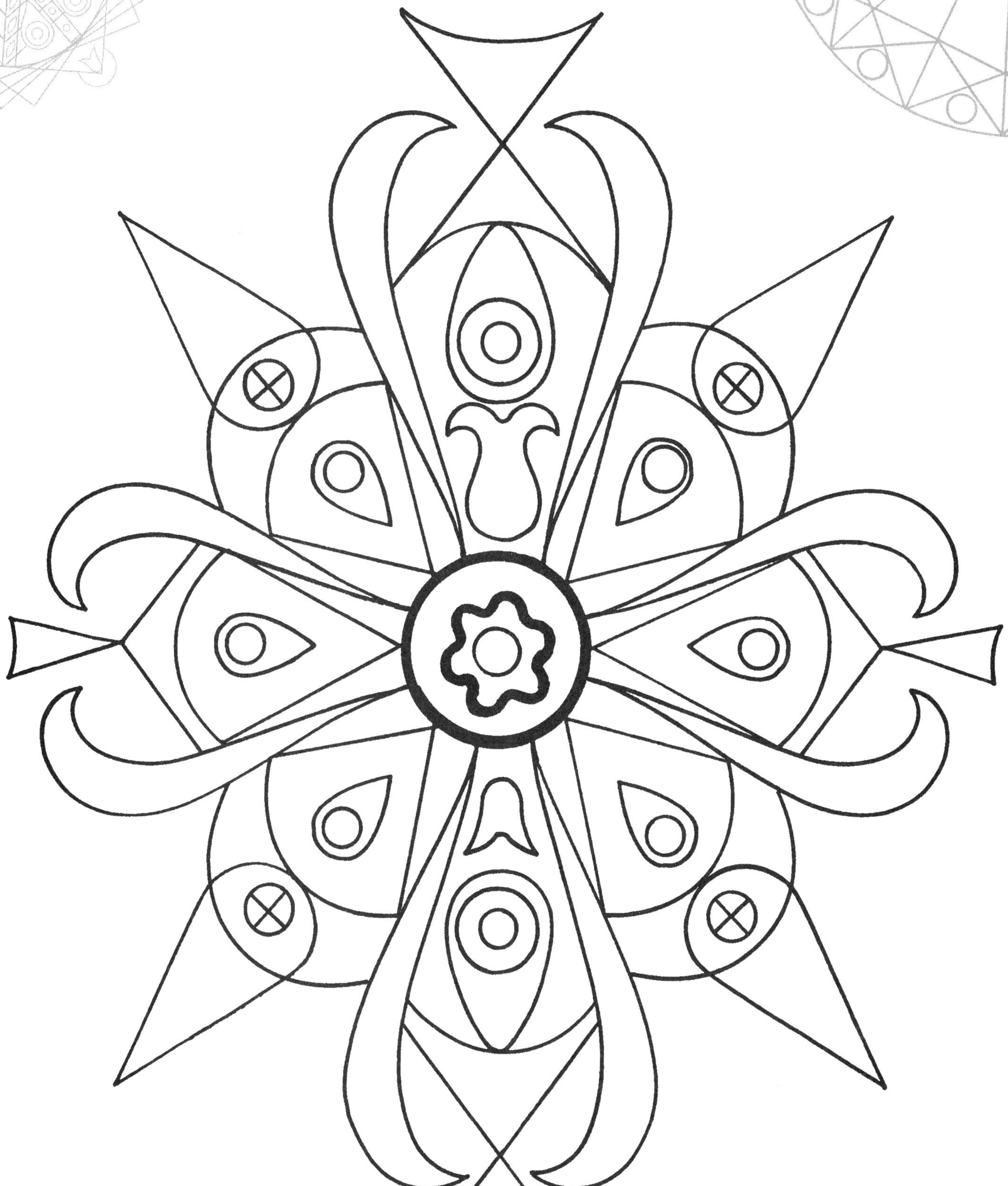

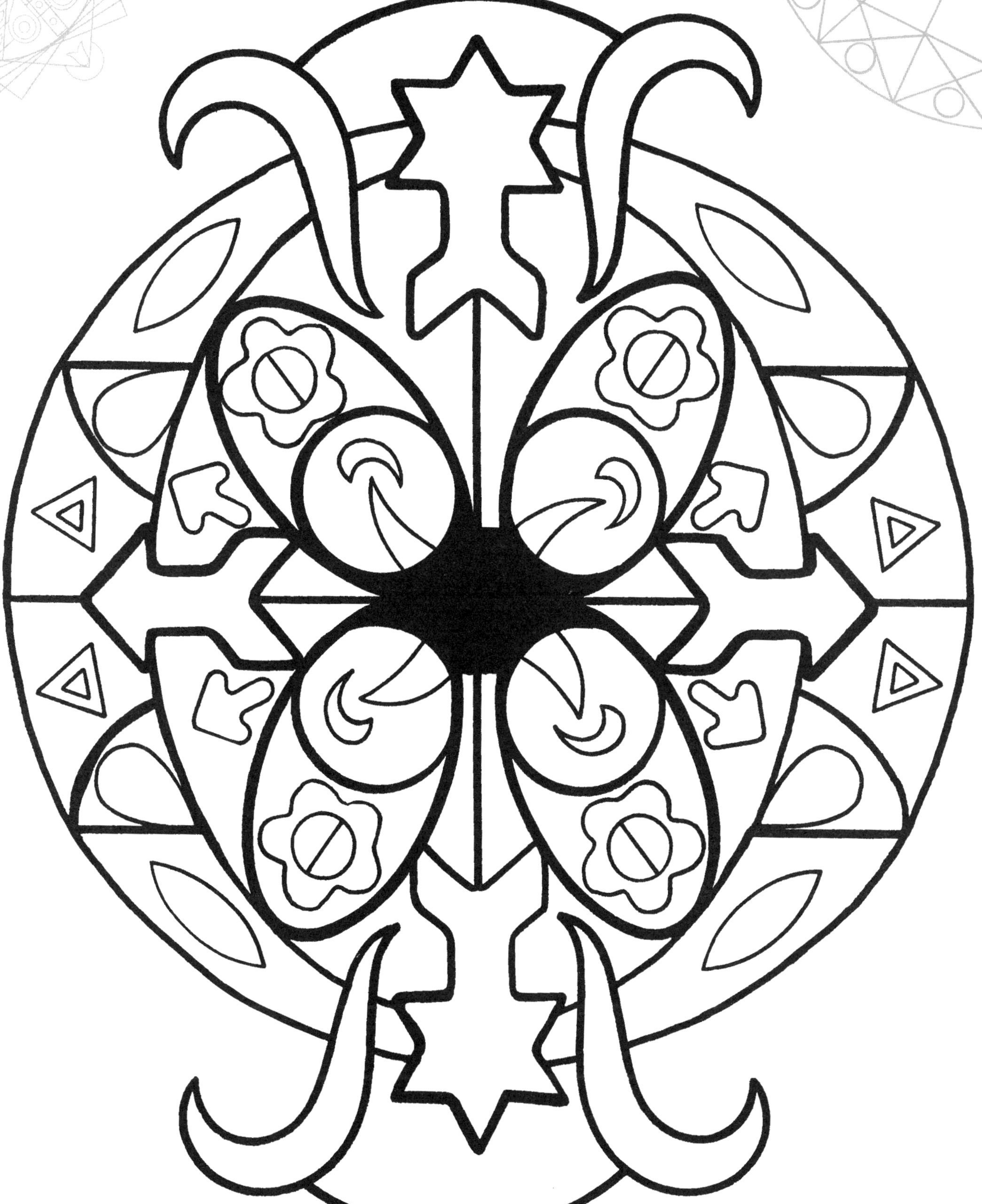

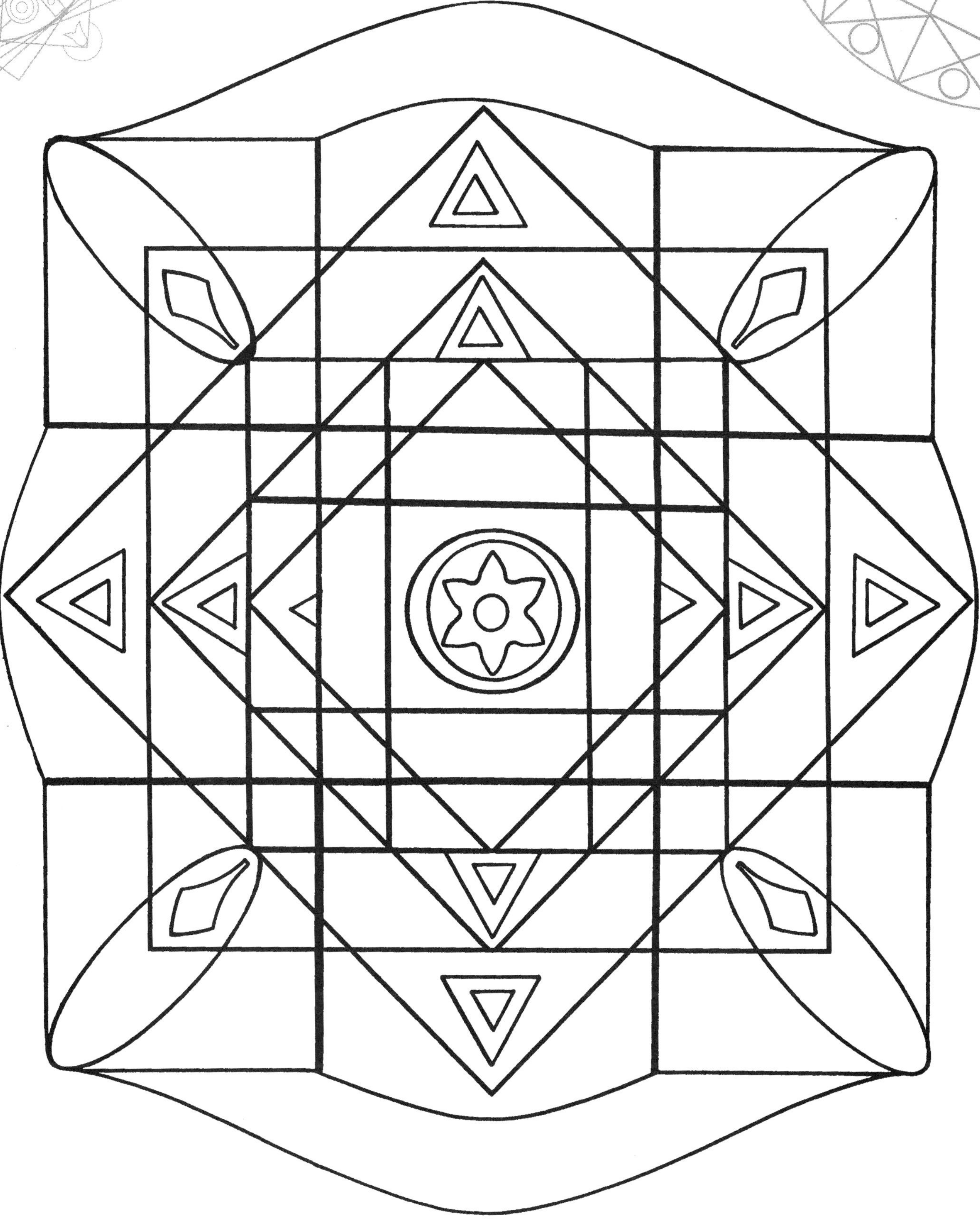

34

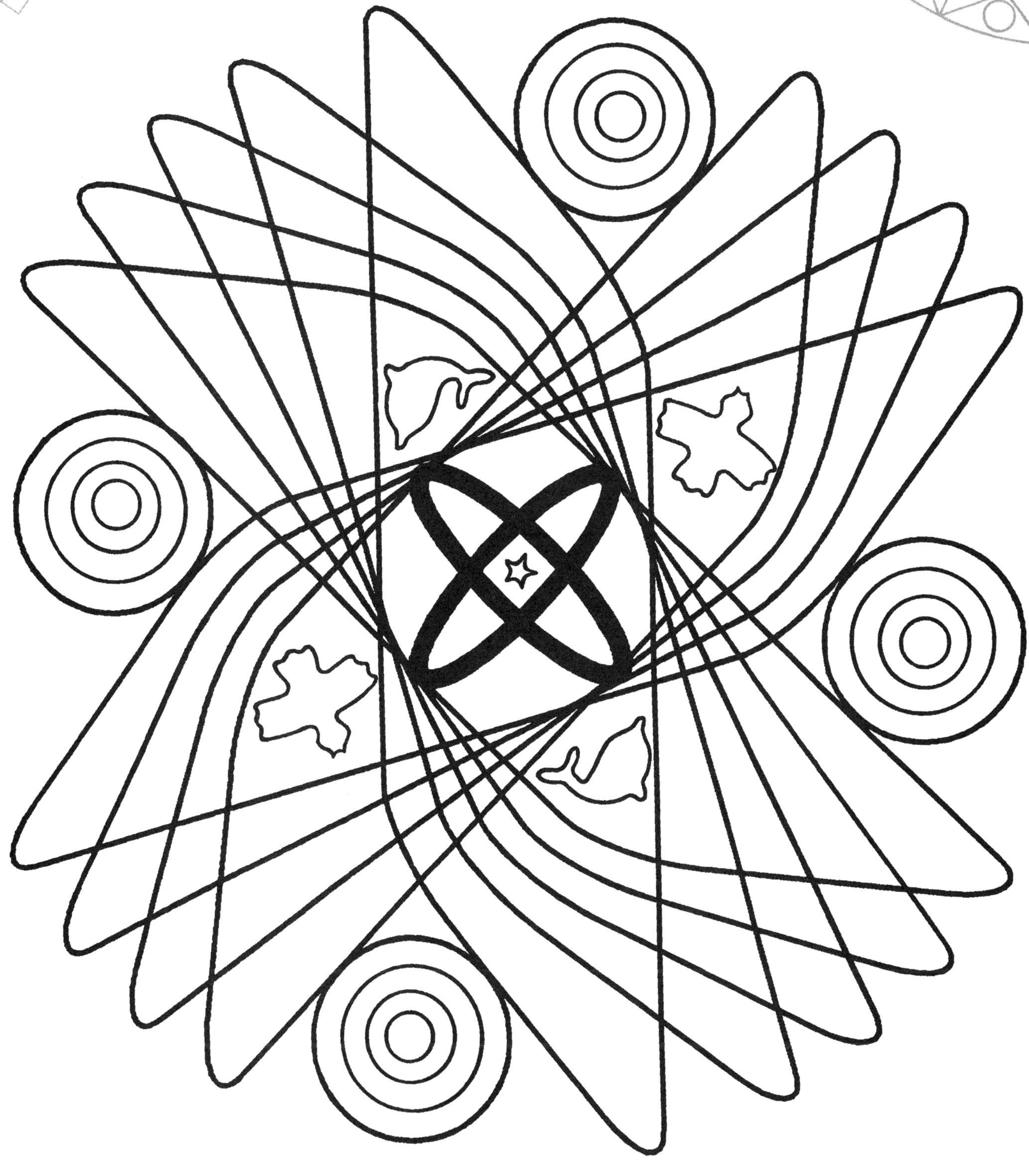

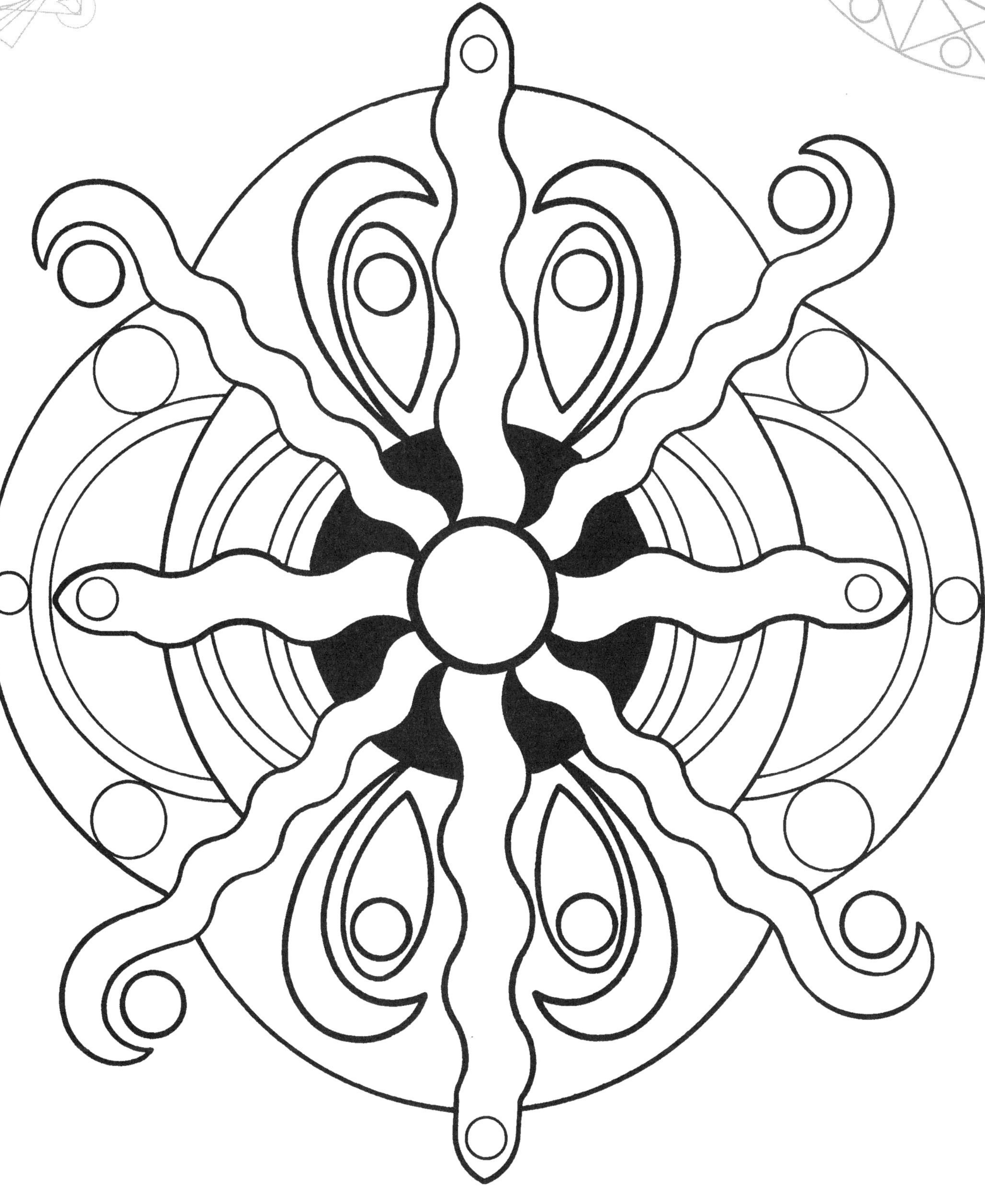

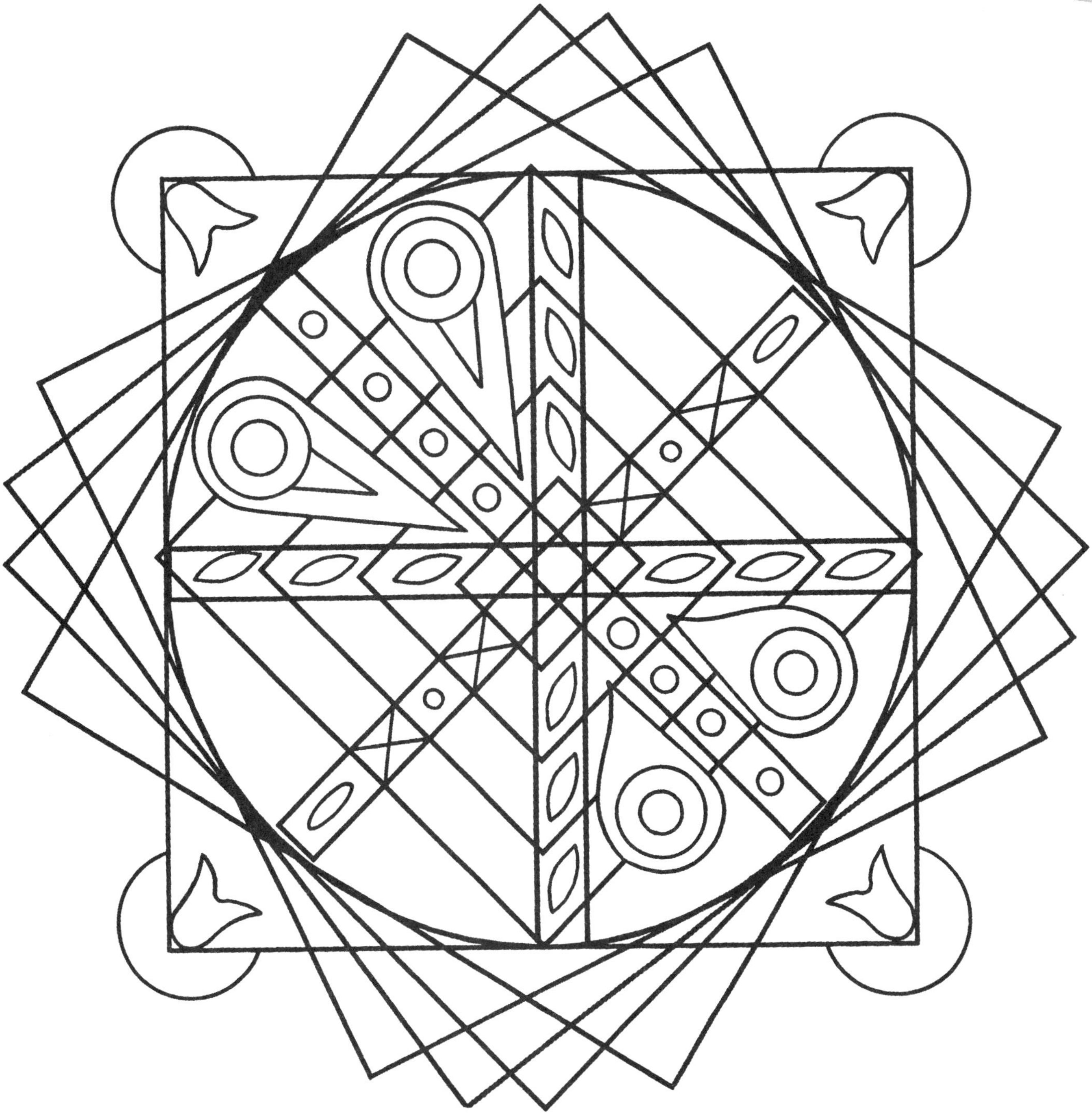

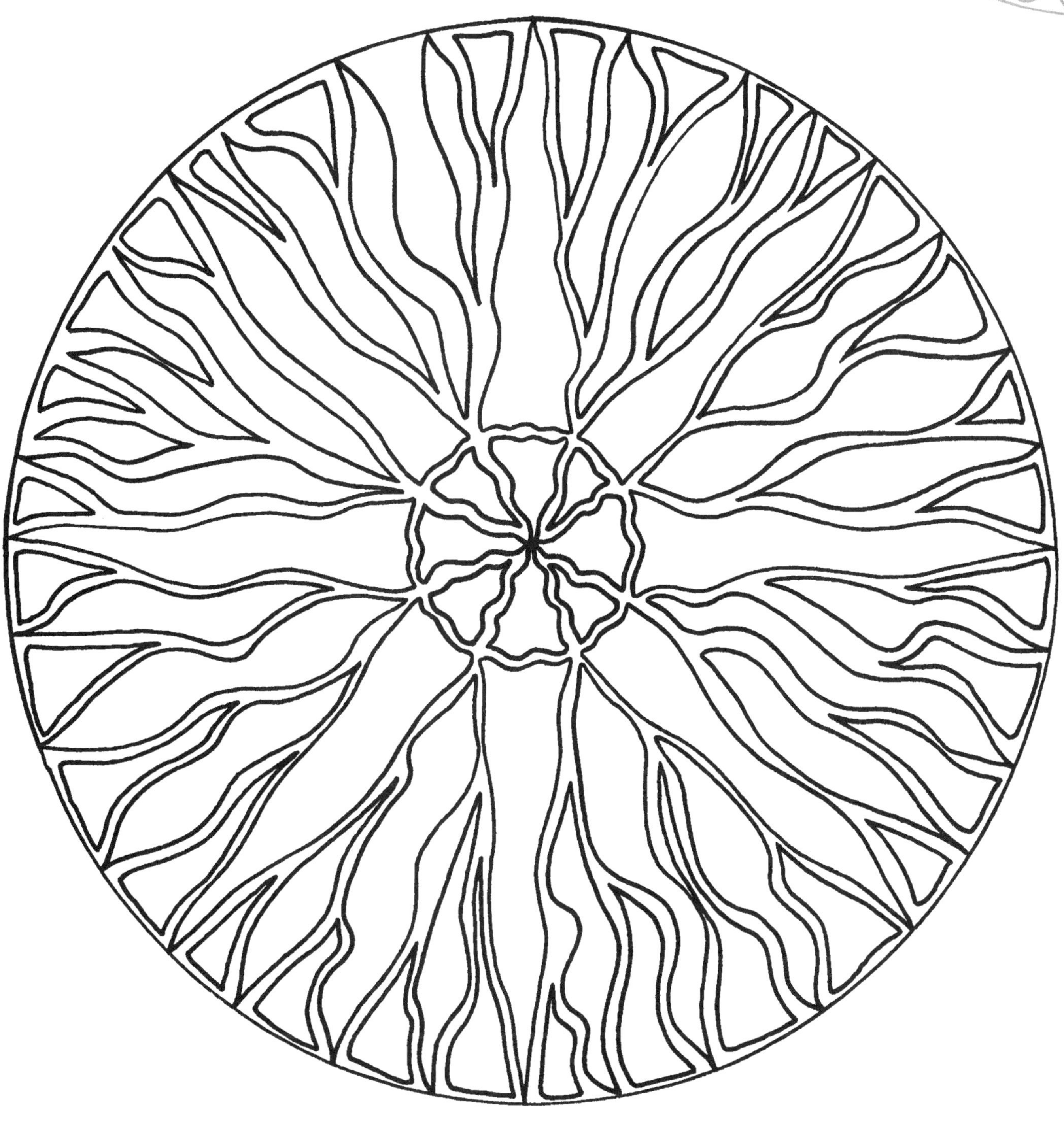

# Magical Mandala Coloring Books from Hunter House

## 42 MANDALA PATTERNS COLORING BOOK

*Wolfgang Hund*

The mandalas in this book are drawn from the entire world of design and nature, mixing traditional designs with modern themes that appeal to children and adults. Nature elements such as trees, moons and stars reflect the environment, while animals such as fish, doves and butterflies remind us we are all part of universal life. Motifs repeat within mandalas in a soothing way that encourages us to revisit the images, finding new shapes and meanings in them. A perfect introduction to the joy of coloring mandalas.

96 pages ... 42 illus. ... Paperback $9.95

## 42 INDIAN MANDALAS COLORING BOOK

*Monika Helwig*

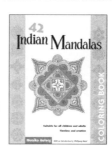

The mandalas in this book are based on ornamental patterns created in households and villages in India. Traditionally made of colored rice powder, flowers, leaves or colored sand, mandalas such as the ones in this book have been used to decorate homes, temples and meeting places. They may be used daily as well as on special occasions, and can be found in the homes of people of all faiths. The artists make each pattern different and special, using all their ingenuity and skill to increase the delight of all who see them.

96 pages ... 42 illus. ... Paperback $9.95

## 42 SEASONAL MANDALAS COLORING BOOK

*Wolfgang Hund*

The mandalas in this book are a mixture of Eastern and Western themes that will appeal to both the sophisticated and the primal in all of us. Luscious fruit, delicate flowers and detailed leaves and snowflakes are among the designs representing summer, spring, fall and winter, while more whimsical patterns include bunnies and spring chicks. You will also find jack-o-lanterns, Christmas scenes and New Year's noisemakers. Children can learn about the seasons and celebrate familiar holidays with these playful, intricate designs!

96 pages ... 42 illus. ... Paperback $9.95

# SmartFun Activity Books from Hunter House

These activity books encourage creativity, concentration, and social activity in children. Appropriate age levels, times of play, and group sizes are indicated for every game. Most games are noncompetitive and none require special skills or training. The series is widely used in homes, schools, day-care centers, and summer camps.

## 101 MORE MUSIC GAMES FOR CHILDREN: New Fun and Learning with Rhythm and Song

*by Jerry Storms*

This book offers a wide array of song and dance activities from a variety of cultures. Besides listening, concentration, and expression games, it includes rhythm games, dance and movement games, relaxation games, and musical projects.

192 pp. ... 30 illus. ... Paperback $12.95 ... Spiral bound $17.95

## 101 DANCE GAMES FOR CHILDREN: Fun and Creativity with Movement

*by Paul Rooyackers*

This book encourages children to interact and express how they feel in creative fantasies and without words in meeting and greeting games, cooperation games, story dances, party dances, and more. No dance training or athletic skills are required.

160 pp. ... 30 illus. ... Paperback $12.95 ... Spiral bound $17.95

## 101 MUSIC GAMES FOR CHILDREN: Fun and Learning with Rhythm and Song

*by Jerry Storms*

This imaginative book is used to introduce children to learning about music and sound. Using audiocassettes or CDs, children and adults get to play listening games, concentration games, musical quizzes, and more.

160 pp. ... 30 illus. ... Paperback $12.95 ... Spiral bound $17.95

## 101 DRAMA GAMES FOR CHILDREN: Fun and Learning with Acting and Make-Believe

*by Paul Rooyackers*

Drama games are a dynamic form in which children explore their minds and the world and use their playacting in sensory games, pantomimes, story games with puppets, masks and costumes, and more.

160 pp. ... 30 illus. ... Paperback $12.95 ... Spiral bound $17.95

*For our FREE catalog of books, please visit www.hunterhouse.com or call 1-800-266-5592. Prices subject to change.*